poems

SKY GILBERT

A NICE PLACE TO VISIT

SKY GILBERT

MISFIT

Published by ECW PRESS, 2120 Queen Street East, Suite 200,
Toronto, Ontario, Canada M4E 1E2
416.694.3348 / info@ecwpress.com

LIBRARY AND ARCHIVES CANADA CATALOGUING IN PUBLICATION

Gilbert, Sky
A nice place to visit / Sky Gilbert.

"A misFit book".
ISBN 978-1-55022-893-9

I. Title.

PS8563.I4743N43 2009 C813'.54 C2009-902547-7

Editor for the press: Michael Holmes / a misFit book
Cover design: David Gee
Author photo: Nicola Betts
Type: Mary Bowness
Printing: Coach House 1 2 3 4 5

The publication of *A Nice Place to Visit* has been generously supported by the Canada Council for the Arts, which last year invested $20.1 million in writing and publishing throughout Canada, by the Ontario Arts Council, by the Government of Ontario through Ontario Book Publishing Tax Credit, and by the Government of Canada through the Book Publishing Industry Development Program (BPIDP).

Canada Council for the Arts Conseil des Arts du Canada Canada ONTARIO ARTS COUNCIL CONSEIL DES ARTS DE L'ONTARIO

PRINTED AND BOUND IN CANADA

ECW PRESS
ecwpress.com

Contents

11 Don't Sleep with Anyone Who
15 Three Approaches to Robert DeParis
19 The Thief
20 The Drama Queen
21 The Old Friend
22 Looking on the Bright Side
24 Ian and Flowers
25 Ode on My Mangina
26 Some Very Funny Things That Might Happen
28 Humouresque
31 I Don't Want to Go to School
33 All Banks Are Death
34 Velly Solly
35 The Kiss at the Door
36 Auntie Louise
38 I Am Not the Kind
39 Self-Storage
40 Ode to John Wildman
42 You Took the Books
43 Some Little Known Truths About *South Pacific*
45 Agoraphobic Poem
46 New York Diary

49 Ravishing
51 Why?
52 Pardon My Aporia
53 The One I Chose
54 Marjorie Morningstar
57 The Damned Don't Cry!
60 Costa Rica
61 Good Question
62 Being With You
64 What Do We Do About Love?
65 On the Way Back from Connecticut
69 It's Something I Learned a Long Time Ago Playing Chess with Dominic
70 Parker Posey
71 Ian's Getting Drunk
72 Ode to Ian
73 To the Boy Who Sits by the Pool
74 Old Man
76 Key West Regret
77 Laura's Dream

78 Why I Would Rather Chat with a Hamilton Crack Whore than an Old Rich Toronto Lady with a Lap Dog
80 Poem for Keith's Birthday
81 Photos for My Family: The Captions I Never Sent
84 Romance
85 The Performance
87 Queer Manifesto

92 Acknowledgements

For Ian

DON'T SLEEP WITH ANYONE WHO

goes out for lunch with his boyfriend wearing matching
    bicycle shorts
knows how gorgeous they are
doesn't wash, you know, back there
shaves their pubes like a Hitler mustache
is very proud of their job
washes back there too much
thinks you own too many books
says "I'm looking for a dark horse baby" is "our song"
    when you hardly know them
asks you if you are a top or a bottom
needs to get fucked up the ass with a big hard cock
    in order to believe they are loved
buys designer soap
wears cut off tops
wears cut off shorts
cuts you off
wears anything with holes deliberately sewn into it
    to show off body parts
dresses like Robin Hood
keeps looking at the most attractive part of your body
    instead of your face
asks if you are HIV positive
is pre-lubed
wears a rainbow or has a special place in their heart for rainbows
reads Stephen King
pats you anywhere
gets into fights with people he's just met
says he threw his last girlfriend out of a window
is married to anything
grabs your balls as if they were a doorknob and pulls
wants to lick every part of your body
wants to do anything sexual with food
says the words "Care Bear"

inscribes a book of Shakespeare's sonnets to you
wears the comedy/tragedy masks on any part of their person
finds dogs irresistible and stops to pet them because
    it's something Marilyn Monroe used to do
doesn't like women
has more than one celtic tattoo
doesn't like black people
is very "tolerant" of black people
thinks black people are "even nicer than white people, actually"
wears sandals
goes to church regularly
loves their parents more than anybody else
just has to spend a few more minutes talking with his friends
    and then he promises, he promises he'll go
asks you what you like to do in bed
is coming to terms with themselves
has more than one therapist
really wants to tell you their feelings about the music
    that's playing
charms the pants off you ten minutes after meeting
cries alone late at night
does crack
thinks they are uninhibited
wears a hankie that means something
thinks you're hilarious
is anti-abortion
dresses like Cher
has one or two overly large testicles – even if that's your special
    fetish
doesn't want you to lick their dick
doesn't want you to kiss them
won't let you touch their ass
has to turn the lights out to do it
lies on their stomach and puts their ass in the air and says
    "I want you to do it to me"

enjoys watching you eat
has had part of their nose removed because of all the coke
has a weird doll sitting alone in an empty closet
    with a solitary light shining on it
has a telescope in a window that faces another building
is more than ten years younger than you
is a teenager
talks like a teenager
likes to sleep with teenagers
seems very teenager-like
orders a teen burger
is desperately looking for love
enjoys hunting
buttons their shirt up all the way
asks you to take a shit on them
does not consider himself to be like other homosexuals
doesn't usually hang out here
has never been here before
is just here to have a sauna and was surprised
    by all the sexual activity going on
hits you
wears a headband
loves Harry Potter
likes to go antiquing
is dressed up like a horse
thinks he doesn't look over forty
inspects your cock before he sucks it
is carrying a purse but is not in drag
is writing a biography of every famous person who ever existed
wonders why young people act so disrespectfully
would never sleep with anyone over thirty
thinks we've moved beyond all that
is house proud
mentions aliens without a sense of humour
asks why you don't smile more often

asks “was that a joke, or are you serious?”
is wearing a charm bracelet
has an entourage
suggests you try it for the first time
wants to be famous someday
says penis instead of dick
says vagina instead of cunt
never says cunt, penis, dick or vagina
is special friends with the bartender
is in any way associated with L. Ron Hubbard
has recently converted to anything
is known by more than one name
reminds you of any member of your family
you feel sorry for
is down for the weekend
never does this
just listens
never listens
is carrying a bag holding something they call their “equipment”
wears a condom for oral sex
refuses to wear a condom
is too gorgeous to be true
dresses entirely in white
gets turned on by pretending he’s shooting you while you cry out
    in pain and has a suspicious scar on his stomach
    and a Serbian accent
is going a little crazy this weekend
asks you if you know where he can get gang banged
believes sex should only be between equals who love and respect
    each other

THREE APPROACHES TO ROBERT DEPARIS

First Person Monologue

My name is Robert DeParis
I was born in St. Foy, that means faith
my mother, she drove my father to an early grave
my brother Antoine, he brought me to you
you are an angel
Antoine told me about you many years ago
we met in another life, yes?
I think you know what I mean
in fact I know you do
I am technically an emperor
but I don't use the title
my family goes back to Louis the IV
so now you have met someone crazier than you
Robert DeParis
I think you know what I mean
my brother Antoine, I must tell you his story
he was my twin and I was born completely blue
he had a small heart
my heart was beating for both of us
when he came out the umbilical cord
(it was huge, by the way)
was wrapped around his neck eight times
he died
I did not want him to die
I mourned for Antoine
even as an infant
I love Citroën
they really know how to make cars
I am a shareholder, not on the board or anything
I'm not saying that
but I love to look at the cars

they invented everything
before the Americans stole it away
would you like a massage?
you have a bad back
I knew that, how?
Antoine told me
I had a fight with my assistant
Alexander, he gave me grief suddenly
he said he was afraid of me
locked himself in his car and told head office
just because I'm bipolar
a bipolar queen named Robert DeParis
I know Michael Jackson and Joan Rivers
when she smiles too hard
it squeezes her asshole
Michael Jackson has a skin disease
he truly does, he has no melanin
his baby doesn't have any either
they had to keep the baby in a bubble
I was robbed last week
five guys beat me up in the park
the police arrested me
I have to go to court next week
but the police have apologized
here, I'll shave your face
this is Biotherm, it's a cleanser
tightens up the pores
here's some cologne
just close your eyes
have some iced coffee
I am from another planet
do you know what I mean?
I think you do
my name is
Robert DeParis

Nostalgic Second Person

It was on the balcony of The Lookout that I met Robert DeParis
sparkling eyes; big shoes
It wasn't long before he was touching me
telling me what a beautiful man I was
I recognized instantly
this was more than sex
this was an adventure
we were going to go somewhere
together
and we did
to several restaurants
in the end we were walking through Ottawa in the rain
and I was truly afraid
and kind of in love with him, too
so we said goodbye
I thought he would be angry
but I think he was as afraid of me
as I was of him
– afraid of us

Analysis

I have met Robert DeParis many times
there are so many boys who say things that are not true
I want to believe them
and when they are speaking, in fact, I do
they take me to other worlds
they tell me what to do
I follow because I am naturally obedient
I realize that there is a bit of Karla Homolka going on here
I was, after all, in the thrall of Robert DeParis
in his Travelodge room
being shaved and sprayed with cologne
I think it was the argument he had with that guy
in the third bar we went to
when Robert insisted that he knew Neil the owner
in fact, had just talked to him
and the guy said *Neil is in Thailand*
and Robert said yes, I just talked to him in Thailand
now keep the bar open you asshole we just want another drink
the manager appeared
it was very dramatic
everything is very dramatic with Robert
he had to calm down
so he started talking about Antoine
I am drawn to the demons
or the demons are drawn to me
somebody has to love them, right?
demons get lonely too

THE THIEF

Someone told me he was a thief. It appears irrefutable. Now, when he greets me in the morning, his smile seems oily. He makes me suspect everyone. What's behind their cheeriness? (Be wary of those who smile too easily or often. Joy is not perpetual, but guile is forever.) "Good morning, Bill. Thank you, and you have a lovely week, too." Meanwhile, he opens the cash drawer surreptitiously, insinuating his fat hairy hand. For this reason I was, at first, suspicious of Mozart. Surely he could not have been happy all the time? But unlike Bill, I believe Mozart – a defective gene perhaps? – *was* consistently acquainted with happiness.

Should I tell the others? Will I be blamed for not revealing my secret? The coffers will be empty soon. But of course it's always something so much more than money that's lost. Trust . . . Faith . . . The simple recognition in a smile.

THE DRAMA QUEEN

Her brightly dyed hair and gypsy skirt swirls cannot distract us from the lines chiseled into her freckled skin. She should not be so thin. There is something tired, resigned about the movement of her hands. You want to like her and sympathize; but you mustn't. And it isn't simply that she married the wrong kind of man – you know the type, a boaster and a drunkard, charming only to women like her. She is in the wrong profession, too, and will most certainly – I detest cursing anyone, but it's in the cards – at some point suffer serious illness. She is suffering now, as I write this. She always suffers. I have no more sympathy left. When she calls me over, curls a finger, I smile. I defer and gently turn away. And I wish her all the best, honestly I do, knowing she is saving the worst for herself, in a little drawer beside the bed. At night she caresses it and cries.

"This is my secret hurt," she says. "No one will ever understand."

THE OLD FRIEND

When we meet of course it is in the middle of a pressing crowd. His eyes, watering with kindness, reach out in my direction. "It's great to see you," he says. "How are you doing?" And it's almost genuine, except he's won so many awards for his acting. I know I sound suspicious, but he shouldn't have done the pity thing, should have controlled himself, simply not brought that to the table. Pity is always in poor taste. He really is so terribly charming, so of course I say, "Fine." And when he says "We have to get together some time," I naturally agree. He looks older, but so, I presume, do I. Soon the throng has carried him away. It's all too *Les Enfants du Paradis* for words. He is no longer as handsome as Jean-Louis Barrault, but I find myself flattered by his attention. He is, as I have said so many times, a light which shines too brightly – to quote Tennessee Williams. When that light is ferried away, and you are left all alone on the dock, it suddenly seems so very cold . . . But when you get too close, it burns. Oh how it burns.

LOOKING ON THE BRIGHT SIDE

the reason my boyfriend is ignoring me is because he's sick
people don't really care whether you get hard
when I shave my head really close you can't see the grey
those lumps seem very close to the surface
the fact that a lot of people are stupid means that I don't have
    boundary issues
it's nice to live in the kind of neighbourhood where you can sing
    to yourself and nobody cares
anything with piping on the shoulders helps
the guy who rejected me because he didn't want to be my first
    time is now fat and old – and he reads people's fortunes
    at gay events nobody goes to
I'll die before I listen to every piece of music I like
the rug doesn't reach all the way to the window
    but the curtain covers the floor
all of my cats will probably die before I do
David Gest has a reality show
straight people will never understand camp
having few friends means I never feel smothered
not being famous means I can walk into a restaurant
    relatively unnoticed
there's nothing much to burgle
I only wind up limping twice a year
my ass is basically the same
it's a pleasant surprise when people discover I'm not as conceited
    or obnoxious as they thought I'd be
most of my internationally famous friends are also unhappy
pornography never ceases to entertain; poppers are a lot less
    satisfying
I have time to be with myself
I will never run out of obscene novelty items
my boyfriend makes sure I never forget I have a bad memory
you can always count on the weather to be a surprise

everybody dies
most of what you figure out about life
    has already been figured out
people have no idea how much I judge them
there will never be another Alfred Hitchcock
I'm not all that interested in sleeping with anybody under 40
    anymore anyway
it's impossible to choke on an ice cube
my boyfriend will never reveal so much about himself
    that he will cease to be a mystery
my cat doesn't seem to throw up as much
no one really looks at your toes anyway
most of what I read doesn't stick
mostly, people don't mean it
most of the time, you're actually the last thing on their minds

IAN AND FLOWERS

Ian loves flowers –
especially daisies, and sunflowers.
"There's something wrong with the tiger lilies," he says.
(Their edges are frayed.)
I try to explain that's the way they're meant to be.
(Ian expects flowers to be perfect.)
When I pull weeds he screams
"No! That's a flower!"
(I am certain it is not.)
Even rainy days, he asks if they have been watered.
I watch him, kneeling in the plants, examining his work carefully.
He's wearing his black glasses;
they hide his sparkling eyes.
I love him, even when his perfectionism
means he won't allow me to touch his flowers.

ODE ON MY MANGINA
(with apologies to Keats)

true, it is not very much like an urn
but it is after all a receptacle
and it is certainly Grecian
in the historic sense
something we should omit discussion of
in polite company
I discovered it in Montreal
I mean, I always knew it was there
a certain emptiness, a hole, in fact,
that God had put in me,
practically, supposedly to get rid of dinner
but in the wisdom of that late Montreal night
I came to understand
it was given to me so I could give myself
give give give
and forget that what's up front really has no meaning
but competitive spirit
that to lie down and take it
is beyond measure
the greatest of all pleasures
who could have known?
except perhaps the most enlightened of Buddhists
that to rid oneself of desire up front
is in fact to receive everything one wants
out back

my mangina sounds like a palpitation
it has not yet been celebrated by Eve Ensler
so I celebrate it here
in something not quite like a poem

perhaps in what it lacks
it too will become something it has ceased desiring to be

SOME VERY FUNNY THINGS THAT MIGHT HAPPEN

1. I might lose one of my student's papers. (Or all of them – oh my God!)
2. My plane might crash – after an agonizing 15 minutes we'll know we're all about to die. (Always check for a nun on the flight.)
3. I might say the wrong thing.
4. My boyfriend might break up with me because I'm bad in bed.
5. My boyfriend might break up with me because I forgot to get someone to clean the ducts.
6. My boyfriend might break up with me because of something to do with money. (Likely, me spending too much of it.)
7. My boyfriend might break up with me. (There are any number of reasons.)
8. I might leave my laptop on the bus. (The bus driver would just take it – everyone knows they're all thieves.)
9. People might figure out I'm stupid.
10. I might piss myself when accepting an award.
11. The police might raid our house and find all the bad things. (I won't even bother going into the details, I'm sure you can imagine.)
12. I might get nose cancer. I might have to have my nose removed.
13. I might go deaf.
14. I might develop a bleeding ulcer.
15. My boyfriend might have an episode and I won't find the pills in time. He would die and it would be my fault.
16. A student might knock on my office door when I was changing out of my long underwear and I would say just a minute and then open the door quickly, all flushed, and forget to zip up my fly, and he or she would think I was masturbating and report it to the University, and the authorities would call me in, especially the awful, scary dyke department head with the glasses and red hair who hates me already and is always so over

the top fake nice but occasionally has fits, and she would have a fit and accuse me of masturbating in my office, and because I'm honest I would have to say yes I have masturbated in my office (even though I haven't, but I have thought of it, which is just as bad), and I would be fired and it would be in all the papers, and I'd have to come in to clean out my desk and all my so-called colleagues would whisper sadly and my students would all desert me but I'd overhear one beautiful boy saying "Poor Sky." I'd leave the building for the last time in the rain and I'd forget to wear a poncho and all my books would get wet and me too, but I wouldn't mind because I would like dying of pneumonia. After all, it's mainly what homosexuals die of anyway.

17. I'd forget everything.
18. I'd remember everything.
19. I'd be all alone.

HUMOURESQUE

Stars: Joan Crawford, John Garfield

Synopsis: This is a terrible movie. There is no plot. John Garfield is very cute as both a little boy and as a man. When he's little, his father says he'll buy him anything he wants for his birthday and, oddly, Garfield chooses a violin. His father would rather buy his son a baseball bat. When the boy starts practicing, his brother says, "Does he have to play that violin all the time?" Oscar Levant is John Garfield's ugly, wisecracking friend. He is Jewish. Levant tells Garfield, "You're too sensitive." He also says, "Leave your hair mussed, you look pretty that way." But don't worry, Oscar Levant is not a homosexual; he is just a sad, ugly, outsider. Joan Crawford, in contrast, is a sad, beautiful outsider. She is a rich art patron and an alcoholic. She's unhappily married to a weak man with a pencil-thin mustache. When we first encounter her, at least five men are trying to light her cigarette at the same time. This means she's a slut. When she first sees John Garfield playing the violin she is so sexually excited that she tosses her cigarette into a potted plant. "I'm constitutionally given to enthusiasm about nothing," she says. The dialogue in this movie is so terrible, I don't know where to start. As for plot, well, she loves John Garfield; but she hates him too. Especially when he plays "The Bumble Bee." Garfield says, "Some people drink because they're frustrated," trying to psychoanalyze her. "Or because they're thirsty" is Joan's reply. They go horseback riding and she falls off. She says, "I can't fight you, Paul," and they kiss. Later, she throws herself into the ocean. The lousy "Tristan and Isolde" that Garfield plays finally drives her crazy.

Most Memorable Line: "This isn't a two hour trip to Chinatown, this is life."

Most Confusing Line: "I can do anything a brainless man can do and I can do it better!"

Most Ridiculous Lines:

"What good is a woman if she's no use to anyone?"

"I love you so I don't care what I think of you."

"I'm tired of playing second fiddle to the ghost of Beethoven!"

"A French philosopher once listed 300 ways to commit suicide. They forgot one – falling in love with an artist!"

"I hate music! I detest it!"

"I bet you haven't been in many grocery stores, have you?"

"Marry. It's an easy word to say."

"Why do I have to shave every day?"

Review: I know I didn't do very well on the synopsis but frankly there was nothing much to synop. What is Joan Crawford's problem here, other than the fact that she is Joan Crawford? The reason I hate this movie is that it gives outsiders a bad name. It's as if being an outsider is about throwing your drink against the wall after saying psuedo-profound things. I've spent my whole life being an outsider and I'll tell you what it really means – it means you just don't understand how other people can be happy doing and talking about mundane things in the face of death. Outsiders aren't people who drink too much because they're horny and happen to fall in love with the wrong people. Outsiders are nuts because they are obsessed with death. After all, death has just as much truth to it as life. This movie is not really about outsiders. It was created to contrast the perfect wholesome life of an immigrant grocer (the innocent, poor John Garfield) against the fancy, soulless, immoral world of high culture (John Garfield the tortured violinist). But like all Joan Crawford movies, it's ultimately about your proximity to a grocery store. "I don't want to spend the rest of my life living over a store," says young Garfield. If only he'd stayed at home with his parents and his father had bought him a baseball bat and he'd married his childhood sweetheart . . . My aunt said to me the other day, "You know, three of my nieces and nephews married their childhood sweethearts when they were seventeen. And they're still married to them. Isn't that something?" I'll say it's something – something that makes me sick.

Number of Asterisks: -2500

I DON'T WANT TO GO TO SCHOOL

I know I should grow up and be responsible, after all I'm meeting
Mary Ball on Tuesday.
I wish her name was Balls.
I refuse, I just refuse to get old inside; and who
is going to make me anyway?
And who is going to know?
I'll just go around being a boy because I like boy things.
I saw a kid in the train station today, and he was maybe
four years old, and he was pulling around a little
Barbie suitcase and he was Pakistani and he was having a ball.
A pair of balls, even.
And all I could think of was wait till you get older
and you're a fag – because that's what he's going to be,
pulling that Barbie suitcase around.
And you're a Paki because that's what people will call you.
And on top of that he was fat.
The best choice would be for him not to grow up, for a house
to fall on him like the bad witch in *The Wizard of Oz*,
or to just to stay young like me.
So on the outside I'll be doing things like taking out
my dental plate and licking it behind my hands,
and swallowing my Metamucil and taking stairs slowly
– you know, the knees – and trying not to stand under
glaring lights, and going on diets, and applying Bio Oil
deep into my wrinkles before I go to sleep
but inside I'll be Peter Pan.
And balls I'll say, balls to you my boyfriend
you are always telling me that I'm old; your "I'm just turning 39"
smile always there to remind me.
How ancient I am.
I can't wait until you turn 40, I just can't wait
Mr. You Have To Face Reality And Save Money And Get A
Mutual Fund And Prepare For Retirement,

Mr. You Can't Wear Horizontal Stripes Because They Don't Make
You Look Like A Sailor They Just Make You Look Fat!
Yes I'm going to die, you're going to die, we're all going to die.
But the thing you don't know, the little secret I have,
is I'm not going to grow old.
Do you know why?
Do you know what the youngest, silliest, stupidest, least
responsible, most impractical thing in the world about me is?
I love you.
I'm listening to Strauss's *Arabella* and the best part is
at the beginning and sometimes I just go back to it
and play it over and over.
Fuck the end, I just want the duet, where they sing like songbirds.
And who's going to stop me?
I can watch reruns of the British version of *The Office*
forever and ever, even though it makes me neurotic
it still reassures me in some weird, inexplicable way.
I'll walk down familiar streets and I'll remember the boys I kissed.
But I'll walk down new streets, too, and kiss new boys.
Sure, sometimes I'll curl up in my room and read my old plays
and remember what it was like to write them –
but that doesn't mean I'm old inside.
Only I will know how young I am.
And only I will believe me.

ALL BANKS ARE DEATH

I know I shouldn't have yelled at Anne Rowsome
or called the president's office
but I'll never forget the way she glared and said:
"If you could please just try to lower your voice, sir,
we can discuss this rationally and calmly."
No, we can't, Anne.
My transaction has been rejected
and it seems so terribly personal.
Banks are like death.
Cold, impervious, persistent.
They are the Not I of oppressive, motiveless malignancy –
minus the motive seeking.
They would gleefully strangle you and then order a coffee.
"Mr. Gilbert has just died while waiting in line.
Could you close his accounts?"
"Yes we can, but the computer won't register it until tomorrow."
"I don't think, at this point, it will make any difference."
God made banks and customer service reps
that we might know death.
Have you passed the threshold?
Seen the tunnel?
The very whitest of light?
Well, my heart stopped beating;
I have dealt with Anne Rowsome
and lived to tell the tale.

VELLY SOLLY

My uncle is a very kind man
I repeat, my uncle is a very kind man
I asked him for the thousandth time if I could see
    those photographs from the war
Because he was so handsome
He pretended that he didn't know where they were, as usual,
    which sent me off, spiralling, typically, thinking
he must *know* that I believe he looked cute in his sailor uniform
    and he certainly doesn't want his fifty-year-old
    homosexual nephew getting off on that
And when I think about it, the whole idea is pretty perverted, I
    mean, getting off on your own uncle as a gangly adolescent
    (he had big ears)
But it's not that
When I finally do find the album it's slender
(the way my uncle used to be)
not even hidden, at the bottom of the pile
There are lots of pictures of cute young sailors,
    including my uncle,
and pictures of the bulldozer he used to operate on Tinian
and then, towards the back, it's there:
the reason he didn't want us looking through the album
Photos are of Nagasaki, after the bomb
Underneath one, my uncle, the teenage sailor, scrawled
"Velly Solly"
And then, under a photograph of a decimated street, he wrote
"It sure doesn't look like New York!"
I want to take the album and run
Because it's certainly a record
of something
I repeat
my uncle is

THE KISS AT THE DOOR

Why do I hesitate?
There is no doubt that you are sure
about something –
though I'm not sure what it is.
You even help me with my bag.
(What fresh tenderness is this?)
Through, or despite, it all,
I insist upon continuing
to believe. It's like every religion,
just as hopeless
and certainly as beautiful.
And this is me talking,
someone who recently e-mailed
someone denouncing faith
as an epistemological tool.
And yet when you turn ever so slightly
after we so crankily lunched out,
(oh the deluge, the children at a proximial table
who screeched and hurled chopsticks
after consuming the unwise mountain of sugar
their mother dumped in their cold Vietnamese tea)
and let me touch you ever so gently
even when your shoulder hurts
I believe you are happy –
not because I must leave
but because I will most certainly be
coming back.

AUNTIE LOUISE

I want to grow up to be like Auntie Louise
I sure as hell do
I want to cancel dinner when it doesn't happen when I want
And I want it to happen at 4 p.m. exactly
I don't want it at noon
Why? Don't ask me why!
I'll tell you – that would make it lunch and I don't want lunch
I want dinner
I already had to give up Christmas
because of your father
so you can damn well eat when I say
And don't expect ham or chicken or a fucking roast
you're going to get finger foods
What do I mean? Don't you know what finger food is?
What kind of a nephew are you?
I mean little deep fried flaky mushroom things
and sausages wrapped in pastry
and okay, alright, cheese
If you're good, I'll let you have some cheese
I also want to grow up to be Auntie Louise
because of what she said about Joy
I just met Joy in the supermarket, she said
But, she said, I looked the other way
Joy is a friend she just had a fight with, but still
It says so much
I want to be like Auntie Louise
and fight with everyone and hate everyone
everyone does everything wrong except for me
and I'm going to sit in my apartment
and drink and smoke myself to death
and when I die you'd better arrange a good funeral
and you'd better visit me in the hospital before I go
You'd better love me

At least pretend
No, I don't care if you want to come, just come
Do you hear me? Spend time with me,
whether you like it or not
And fix the curtains
Fix the curtains while I tell you
how much I used to be desired
by so many men, and how I only like to give
certain men blowjobs
– only when I am in love –
and then I'll tell you how bad my husband was
in bed for the thousandth time
While I tell you you can wash the floor
Or else I'll cry
Why? Why? Because I feel suddenly sad and lonely
I don't know why
Why can't I wash the floor?
Don't ask stupid questions
I'm old and I can't move
and I'm your Auntie Louise
Jesus, you are a rude little bastard sometimes
Yes Auntie Louise, whatever you say
I want to grow up to be just like you

I AM NOT THE KIND

I am not the kind who breakfasts with the other guests
Downstairs, they are laughing
The smell of cinammon buns wafts past my room
But I can't imagine a torture more severe
than joining them for coffee
I'm not really a visitor, just a paying guest
But the truth is their conversation
not only bores me but drives me crazy
because it's the little lies, after all
that ultimately kill you
the number of times you say
"The french toast is delicious"
when you would rather not have blueberries
at all – that kind of lie
It has something to do with smiling
when you lie
your heart must pull your eyes up into smiling position
out of decorum
(lest you be left with an obviously fake smiling face
mouth grinning, eyes sagging)
The neurological result is a perilous strain
No, I am not one who breakfasts, cheerily
and sets out on my jaunty way
Bye all! Have a nice day
Sue, don't forget to buy those mittens!
Canadian winters are cold!
These lacerating inanities
I wish I could say I was above them
But the truth is they just hurt
It's still language, after all

SELF-STORAGE

I've had my self in storage
it's time to take it out
The cranky old proprietor isn't shy about complaining
"My back hurts. All this trouble, for what?"
(there's no point explaining that his back is not my problem)
as he opens the door
I was expecting cobwebs, a bad smell
Instead, it's like I never left
A gramophone plays Offenbach
a box of Cheez-Its and a statue of Katharine Hepburn
a pornographic chess set
eyeglasses that let you to see just one thing at a time
The Game of Life spread out on the coffee table
and you, sitting in the corner
"What took you so long?"

ODE TO JOHN WILDMAN

I am in your place
doing nothing
except writing this
(which I am trying to make
as much like nothing as possible)
John, you lent me your apartment for the weekend
but the ceiling is falling
and the toilet tank must be manually refilled
and the bed leaning against the wall almost fell on me
and there's an awful lot of dust
Yes, it's still an apartment
in fact, I'm gazing out the window right now
– all apartments have windows
though some more than others –
and I know that soon, somewhere, the sun will set
Thank heaven the crazy lady with the ferret left
I remember how you reassured me
"A ferret is really an awful lot like a cat"
O John Wildman
to know you is such a pleasure
because when we first met twenty years ago
you were starring in the great Canadian
film called *My American Cousin*
and picked me up in that big red convertible
("My friend lent it to me – for the movie," you said)
Now, so many years later, as I lay
down to sleep in your bed (that almost killed me)
I notice your Genie lying beside my head
casually on its side, as if also trying to sleep
(a Genie looks something like a man)
which is what we all are, really
and I think of how Zen it is of you
to leave it in this falling-down apartment

The Dean Moriarty in me wants to take it
– to see if you'll notice
(it's a Jack Kerouacish life we lead)
Who knows how we'll end up
or how we'll meet in another twenty years
I'm sure I'll hear your voice on the phone
"Hey Sky . . . It's The Wildman here"
(I've always hoped you'd live up to your name
and you kind of do
and that's all we can really hope for, isn't it?)

YOU TOOK THE BOOKS

We were waiting to go to couples therapy
when you saw a box full of old books
You had to stop and look
What about this one? This?
No, we don't want that . . .
We wound up with *Bartlett's Familiar Quotations*
(From Marcus Aurelius to Mae West)
and *On Being and Becoming Human*
by Willard Gaylin
also *Boundaries and Boundary Violations in Psychoanalysis*
by a man and a woman who were both M.D.s
(I know you were particularly fond of the last)
I said "There's lots of Shakespeare in the Bartlett's!"
and you replied "Well that would make for a lovely evening
you can read to me your favourite quotes"
You were being sarcastic
I thought about boundaries and how important they are to you
I opened up the boundary book and read
"Some analysts seem to have a masochistic investment
in their own suffering"
I'm not going to even try to explain why that is relevant to us
because it might start an argument
– the same old argument, all over again –
When our appointment was over
you started looking at me funny, saying
"Am I your Mommy? Would you like to call me Mommy?"
That was fun
But I will always remember that you stopped at the book box
and that you just had to see what was inside

SOME LITTLE KNOWN TRUTHS ABOUT SOUTH PACIFIC

1. I am Nelly Forbush.

2. It does happen across a crowded room. And if it doesn't, it should. And if it never has, it should be capable of happening that way someday. That is, if it's really love.

3. Bali Hai is a house of prostitution. Or at least an island with a house of prostitution on it – that's where the young sailor goes to get fucked. The girl he fucks is being sold by her mother who has a beautiful song called Bali Hai and he falls in love with the girl and wants to rescue her and take her away from that island of prostitution. And Bali Hai is the place we all wish we were, our favourite, fantasy place. Its other name is Costa Rica.

4. Just outside of San Jose in Costa Rica, in the suburb of Rohrmoser, the houses are big and beautiful, but they are all protected with iron fences and sometimes even with barbed wire. You have to drive through the poor neighbourhoods on the edge of town if you're going to the bathhouse, and those neighbourhoods are very scary. When you get to the bathhouse it's called Paris and it seems like an historic building. When you get inside there is a lovely little hall with a pretty picture of a nude man on it. But when you really get inside you are in some 19th century vision of hell. The dark rooms haven't been cleaned in ages (watch out don't slip and fall!) no hot water, no soap, ugly men walking around in towels, stains on the walls, the beds ripped up – piss shit sperm – ugh, probably disease. But I met the most beautiful boys there. That's where you meet the most beautiful boys. Which is why they call it Bali Hai. Also Paris.

5. Ian won't let me in. I am knocking at his door. I am knocking and I am saying Ian I am here and I love you and I know I'm not perfect – which he keeps reminding me. There's a part of him that he

always keeps safe and locked away. I'll love him even if he never opens the safe (he has the key), but I would rather he opened it up and let me in. Do you think it might happen, and if so, when?

6. We will get our little house in Costa Rica and there will be a place for me to write poems like this and a place for Ian to make art. At night we will go downtown and have our pecadillos, or sometimes we will stay home and make out. No one will know that we are there. Or maybe they'll know, but they won't care – and that's the way we'll like it. And Ian will go white-water rafting and have adventures with white boys that he talks to and I'll have dark silent boys to make love to or maybe I'll learn their language. Who knows?

7. *Happy talky-talky happy talk. Talk about things you like to do. Hey, you gotta have a dream you gotta have a dream. Or else how you gonna to make a dream come true?* That's what the little Asian girl sings in *South Pacific*.

8. My uncle built the runway for the Enola Gay, the plane that dropped the bomb on the Japanese.

9. It's so wonderful and life is so sweet and we're all just really the same colour, aren't we? But, excuse me, what is that colour?

10. Purple flowers, mountains, clouds, palm trees in the wind. In December it rains in the middle of the afternoon for a few seconds, and then it's gone.

11. It's a nice place to visit but I would want to live there.

AGORAPHOBIC POEM

It's one of those summer days
when the heat and humidity
is gathering for a torrential downpour
I've decided I love the rain
It's is a new decision
(like loving Graham Greene)
On sunny days I am clear like glass
and everyone can see inside me
It's not fair and I'm afraid
It's not my organs (everybody has them)
but my wishes and fears and perversions
and what I do wrong and can't remember
and my inadequacies
and what I must measure up to
No one wants to be made of glass
(I categorically refuse to be Laura's unicorn)
So I love rainy days now
and I'm in the back room of the old library on College
(it used to be the boys and girls library, but now it's novels)
and there's a little chair in the corner
where I can curl up
and no one knows who I am
or what I'm doing
or what I like or don't
and it's none of their business
anyway, it really isn't
so there
Outside: the storm rages
I'm content
waiting for the end of the world

NEW YORK DIARY

1.
The skateboarders on the train platform are the antidote
Who cares about terrorism
as long as one has blonde hair and the other black skin
and they put their arms around each other for a picture?

2.
I watch them
and they don't realize
because I'm old

3.
It certainly doesn't seem the same in Chelsea, though
I'm off the train and on the street in five minutes
and the boys are trying to pick me up
I'm so happy because one stops
his entire gang of friends
"You're cute," he says

Okay, yes, I'm bragging
Why shouldn't I?

4.
Sex is always where you least expect it
for years I've been going to the bathhouse
but it turns out there's a video store
beside The Barracuda
where all sorts of things happen

If you can't find anybody to have sex with
look right under your nose

5.
What is intimacy?
I think that it all has to do with whether or not
you care if you squeeze their eyes out
Once I squeezed my boyfriend too hard
and his contacts popped out
Now I worry every time I squeeze him
what will happen?
With other boys I don't worry what pops out

With intimacy comes complication

6.
There are so many policemen
and so many businessmen
it's hard to make myself worry about them
being blown up
even by fundamentalists
who I don't like
fundamentally

7.
I was thinking about bill bissett
and Ellie, who has been bleeding
out of her bumhole lately
both of them make me want to be a better person
bill because people look at him oddly
when he calls them "Mr. Steve"
Ellie because she's just, well, Ellie
and who knows what pink and blue outfit
she's going to turn up in

8.
I thought I saw Dominick Dunne
on the train to Connecticut

but it turned out to be
another half-dead, red-faced
far too white old man

9.
If my computer is blown up by a terrorist you won't be able to
read this

10.
Krispy Kreme Doughnuts

RAVISHING

I really am worried that I'm turning into my father
that there is no difference really between him and me
after all we're both old
and we like to show off
and put lampshades on our heads at parties
and people are scared of us
but there's nothing to be scared of
and we both have a swell sense of humour
But there's one important difference
I was at my father's house one sunny day eating breakfast
and there out the window I saw
a very muscular, tanned teenager bent in the garden
"Who's out there?" I asked
"The gardeners" said my father
"I have to get them to order some red mulch
though I will say, it's more expensive"
Shades of Lady Chatterley
– there were three of them
One was dark and dangerous-looking
with thick arms and pants that were falling off
then there was the lanky one with the blond curls
who sort of bounced around
and another one
I can't remember, but he was beautiful too
And it struck me that they were like flowers
and that this was the difference between my father and me
He was trying to interest me in the breakfast conversation
while my eyes kept wandering
and I thought
He knows that I am attracted to these
young men, his gardeners
And I suddenly wanted to be the soil
to lie flat on the ground and have them

do whatever it was they felt necessary
Oh dear, it's not that my father
is not conscious of sex
after all he begat me
and there's the poster in the basement
of the girl in a tennis skirt
with her cute little ass exposed
but somehow that's not the same thing
I am one of those born to be ravished
and it seems that if I am not on a regular basis
or at the very least occasionally
then something's sadly lacking
I cannot imagine my father being ravished . . .
and not just because he is my father
Yes, the difference
definitely has to do
with ravishment
Actually, I am more like my mother
My father will live to be very old
but I will never forget my mother
puffing hard on her cigarette
"I want quality, not quantity" she said
It's important to remember that
to each his own
My father does not need to be ravished
My mother would like to be ravished by a cigarette
and me, well, someday my mulch will come

WHY?

Explain why I wasn't supposed to lick
that boy's asshole last night
(I've had the Hepatitis shot, twice)
Please help me understand what was wrong
about kissing his cute mouth and gazing into his dark eyes
and running my fingers through his curly hair
It's also important for me to remember why
I shouldn't have swallowed his hard dick
or caressed his washboard abs
or watched him come
so happily over his own chest
I also want to know why it was bad
to wish each other Merry Christmas
I know it was wrong to have so much fun
especially during the holidays
I even know I'm supposed to feel
sad or lonely or something
But thinking about it just makes me want to do it again
So please, if you can, just remind me
Why?

PARDON MY APORIA

I'm afraid I won't be able to make the cloning
but I certainly don't want to miss the reception
Forgive me if I'm late for the colon replacement
but Miranda has invited me to pee
If I arrive too late for the disembowelment
please forge some pithy parsing
If I miss the catechresis, don't cry
I've got an amanuensis coming
If I do not attend the weeping party
don't consider it a wet indication
of malenfranchised disembarkment
I'm just busy
If you finally do wane
I'll make every effort
Unless it's time to dump
If, in fact, the embellishment lasts too terribly long
I may just skip out and drop in at the crisis
You keep saying everyone was talking
at the initial psoriasis ritual
but I can't help that
After all my yarmulke keeps scrimping
And surely you know how it is
when there's just no diegesis
– unless you felch
which I absolutely refuse to do
unless the gap inducer is in season
(which I know it isn't)
Where is diachronic Javid when you need him?
Anyway, have a Happy Pilcher
and when it's done say misty for me
over Siltdown's creatin destroyer
(I do so hate when he minches)
And give my love to Sandy
– if he hasn't penetrated yet

THE ONE I CHOSE

You were the one
that's the way it goes
a rose by any other name
I thought you were a nice guy
I had no idea you had a sleep disorder
and Wolff-Parkinson-White Syndrome
and, well, a lot of other things too
Where do I begin?
I mean there's dyslexia
general irritableness and crankiness
and terminal messiness
punctuality issues
(Having to be early, always –
at least we're the first to get to the hors d'oeuvres)
and control issues and style issues
(you think I talk too much and too loudly)
and all the things that drive you crazy about me
(like the way I tap my foot
– even when I told you that my grandfather did it, too
you said genetics was no excuse
so we might as well add coldness and cruelty
and emotional brutality to the list)
And that's just the beginning
but you are the one I chose
So now I'm stuck with you
and I don't mind, for many reasons
but mainly because you hate the same movies
and lean over to kiss me
and it's like you're reaching up
even though you're as tall as me
The best way I can explain it
is that you love the world
and hate it at the same time
which just seems the way it should be

MARJORIE MORNINGSTAR

Stars: Gene Kelly and Natalie Wood

Synopsis: Natalie Wood plays a shallow teenager, very convincingly. Gene Kelly is a little less convincing as a tortured artist named Noel Airman (so named because he is terribly empty inside). But Carolyn Jones is the most convincing of all as the ugly best pal whose eyes are too far apart for her to ever really be pretty. "I didn't want much. Just a friend, a job and a fella," she says. "Aren't I supposed to have feelings? What am I? A lizard?" It's true, Carolyn Jones was not meant to have feelings – that's why she wound up playing Morticia on *The Addams Family* (really, her best part). The plot of this movie is very involved. It goes on and on, but it can also be summarized up in one sentence: Natalie Wood is madly in love with Gene Kelly, but she never gets him. Natalie is a pretty Jewish teenager with strange, dangerous, inexplicable yearnings – so she goes to teach drama at a kids' camp. Her mother doesn't approve. Her funny looking, sexually promiscuous, yet somehow endearing, best friend Marsha Zelenko (Jones) sneaks her off to a resort called South Winds. That's where she meets Noel Airman. He's trouble. "You don't belong here Marjorie, go home," he says. He kisses her. It's downhill after that. Noel Airman is no good, but of course she loves him anyway. Perhaps because of it. Her nice Jewish parents come to watch Natalie perform at the resort. At first they approve of the tasteful Spanish dance she's doing, but suddenly Natalie whips her black skirt off and she's bouncing around singing Rock, Rock, Rock! wearing nothing but a sequined leotard. No, they don't like that at all. In order to secure Marjorie's love, Airman suddenly quits being a tortured artist and becomes an ad exec. "I'm sick of trying to figure out who I am and why I'm here and what it's all about," he says. (Hamlet could learn something from this guy.) But it doesn't work. At the movie's climax he becomes a tortured artist again, taking self-sabotage to new heights, yelling at potential Broadway backers, "Success covers you like a coat of grease! You're disgusting! Why don't you walk out on me!" Then, he starts crying. Natalie Wood dumps him and then just narrowly escapes marrying Martin Balsam. (Doesn't everybody?) In the end she marries a dull, ugly playwright with glasses, giving up her dreams of being a glamorous movie star to please her nice Jewish Parents.

Most Ridiculous Line: "I have a fatal lack of central organizing energy."

Review: Pardon me while I puke. I did have one revelation, though. Why is it that most of the actresses in these movies are so lousy, even if they're good? I mean Natalie Wood is just a terrible actress, as bad as Lana, but even Joan Crawford and Bette Davis were forgettable in these potboilers. Why oh why, I ask myself, why? The answer is: because most of these trashy movies are about women who give up acting careers and romance and passion for a boring family life – so, if the actresses were actually good it would be too scary for the women watching the movies. The women watching these movies wanted to see normal, unthreatening women like themselves, not women like Tallulah Bankhead, who have at least three cunts and a tiny penis to boot. "It's all very Brechtian, don't you know?" Women didn't really want to get emotionally involved with these movies, they just wanted to have the values of their comfortable world confirmed, which meant watching some lousy actress go through the paces half asleep. That's Natalie Wood's speciality. Do you know how Natalie thinks in movies like this? She cocks her head. Yes, in any Natalie Wood movie, you will find her cocking her head at the moment of revelation.

Number of Asterisks: Have I become too analytical here? *Marjorie Morningstar* and Bertolt Brecht in the same sentence? Come on – when Gene Kelly first meets Wood he calls her "Morningstar." Natalie Wood goes, "Umm, but my name is

Marjorie Morgenstern." Right, she's eighteen years old and her quite obviously over-European parents have *never* told her what her name means in German? Did anyone really believe this crap when it first came out?

THE DAMNED DON'T CRY!

Star: Joan Crawford

Synopsis: Joan Crawford buys her son a bicycle. Her cheap, insensitive husband wants her to take it back. They fight. Joan Crawford just wants her kid to have fun. What's the harm in that? Sure sometimes fun costs a little money. While his parents argue, the kid gets hit by a truck. Joan leaves her penny-pinching husband. She gets a job modelling clothes for a sleazy fashion company. She has to go out to dinner with the buyers and let them grope her. It's the out of town buyers that are the worst. Joan suddenly gets all hard and tough. She chews gum. She develops a sly smile and her gigantic mouth goes all crooked. She meets a shy young accountant. She turns into Lady Macbeth. "I don't have any nerve," the cute accountant says. "I've got enough nerve for both of us," says Joan. After that it's all downhill – a rollercoaster ride straight to hell, a quick and dirty flight to the middle of a dung-heap, a motorcycle race to the edge of a ring of fire. Joan thinks she's getting what she wants, which is money; but in the process she's damned. You feel sorry for her, because she's just a woman in a man's world. And besides, she tells it like it is: "The only thing that counts is that stuff you take to the bank, the stuff that everybody sneers at but works so hard to get." That's calling a spade a spade in the United States of America. Pretty soon she's wearing slutty dresses and it looks like she's got a pair of hands covering her tits. She's putting on makeup and yelling at the accountant. Then she meets George Castleman, the mobster (that's man number three), and things go into high gear. The mobster sure has her number. They speak to each other in movie talk, the kind of talk that means that people have big erections for each other. Why? Because they can look deep into each other's soul. But we know it's going to end up messy. Joan comes into his office wearing a hat with a big flower and stinking of cheap perfume. The name of her perfume is Temptation. He rips the flower off her hat and says, "A lady never hides her face. Especially a face as beautiful as yours." He kisses her. Joan dumps the accountant and changes her name from Ethel Whitehead to Lorna Hansen-Forbes. Now that she's hyphenated, she thinks nobody can stop her. Things go okay until one day George sends Lorna to get some information on one of his two-timing thugs. The two-timing thug is very hairy and Italian and looks just fabulous in a bathing suit. Instead of getting the information she's supposed to get, Joan falls in love with him. Or maybe she just wants to get boned (that's guy number four). There's no turning back. I mean it's worse than Shakespeare. Pretty well everybody ends up dead. But let's face it, we knew what was coming when Joan didn't mind being groped by the out of towners – we knew she wasn't long for this world. This movie is memorable because Joan Crawford is starting to wear the horrified expression that she perfected in the stupid horror movies that followed. Only in this movie it isn't an axe that's coming at her, it's the American Dream. The accountant has a good line at the end: "No, this isn't a party you can leave when you're bored. We could have left a long time ago. We were the only guests then. But we've stayed too late." That's the moral: don't go out and stay up too late – you might end up shot dead in your own front yard.

Best Scene: When Joan and the accountant are arguing in a cab. The driver is listening and Joan notices. She yanks up the glass that separates the front from the back seat. (Do they still have those things? Did they really ever have them?) And then the driver watches the reflection of them kissing in the rear view mirror.

Most Memorable Line: "Don't talk to me about self respect. That's something you tell yourself you got when you ain't got nothin' else."

Most Confusing Line: "You've got a brain – the best kind! The kind you don't have to go out and buy!"

Review: You think you want a life like this? Lusting after men and money; man after man, dollar after dollar? Where does it get you? It gets you shot on the lawn, that's what. But still, it's better than sitting at home drying dishes. Isn't it?

Rating: Not as good as *Mildred Pierce* but that's mainly because it doesn't have Eve Arden.

Number of Asterisks: I don't know. And I'm not even going to try. What's an asterisk equal to anyway? How much enjoyment? Jesus, enough already with the asterisks.

COSTA RICA

There was fear on the plane
the cockatoos were fighting
we're lost in a third world
through the window I can see purple flowers
I don't know what they're called
I don't really care
You know it's too bad Allen Ginsberg gave contemplation
    such a bad name
I can see the water and the dappled palms
    through the window too
the fags next door are yelling mundane things
I can pretend not to hear
there is a boy sleeping in my bed
there was a boy's cock in my mouth last night
we were looking for the railroad tracks
that was then
this is now

GOOD QUESTION

Is the plant real?
I am touching it
But I can't tell

The hotel could have put it here just to fool the tourists
– there is a part of me that wants to enjoy the plant
but what if Neil were to find out
(that's not his real name)

"Oh, you enjoyed that fake Costa Rican plant
they put out to fool stupid tourists"
he'd say, as if he were God

He's not

I have every right to look at this flower and enjoy it
just as I have every right to love San Jose
even if Dave's sister (not his real name)
said it was a hole

Maybe a hole is what I was looking for

Did you ever consider that?

BEING WITH YOU

Sometimes being with you is like that day I woke up at the gym
after so many years of being fucked in the head
(finally off the drugs, it took me three months to sober up)
Very Bukowskiesque, he said, feeling literary
and suddenly I realized life is very mundane
and time moves very slowly
and there isn't really that much fun at all
on a moment to moment basis
compared to drugs, that is

But I just decided, you know, *this is life*
just accept the boringness of it

By that I don't mean you're boring
because in a *Thin Man* sort of way
there's always bickering
and after all, I'm not you and you're not me
and thank Christ, or whoever's worthy of worship today
it's true, I still cherish your cross-eyed kisses
no matter how hard it is for you to dredge up love
(sometimes I can see you trying
not that you don't want to love me
really, I understand, occasionally,
it's hard to love
anybody, because, well, we both know
life is difficult, but what cheers me up
most of all is, after all, you do bother)

Then there are those moments
like when you realize the grocery store
in this third world country is much better stocked
than the one in our working class neighbourhood back home
– how depressing it all is –

and you run to tell me
That's our Asta
the dog that follows us, wagging its tail
and after all these years, he's still barking

WHAT DO WE DO ABOUT LOVE?

After eight years we just got to the point where we decided it was alright for you to tell me about the guy that you used to go-kart with and have sex with – and I have to be open-minded about it. (Just imagine what *you* have to put up with – we won't go into that now.) His name was Alan and he was married and bisexual and his wife didn't know about you, except she met you once and you lied and pretended you were just Alan's friend – which you were, in a way, when you look at it all very open-mindedly. I know Alan was not your intellectual equivalent, no competition for me, and that the fact he was an ex-cop and had shot a man's legs off just happened to give you an erection (over and over, time after time). I understand that. (Please don't ask me why, but I do.) And I realize you had to end your friendship when Alan's wife caught him talking dirty to you on the phone. Apparently she was really mad. What did she say to him, I wonder? ("You'd better stop talking dirty to that beautiful boy with the sparkling eyes right now, you'd better stop or else I'm getting a divorce!") But maybe they had been together for eight years too. Maybe it even became a fantasy for them. Like last night, when you pretended I was your Costa Rican servant and you spanked me for not washing the floor correctly. After eight years, gee whiz, it's all very strange, isn't it? I mean, what do we do about love?

ON THE WAY BACK FROM CONNECTICUT

1.
June had a tiny cough, or rather she covered her mouth when she coughed so it sounded like a hiccup and her little body jumped, and then she apologized. She was my aunt (sort of, but not really) and she gave me a book. I remember it was raining all the time and she said, "It's called *The Catcher in the Rye* and it's rather risqué." I was twelve and we were in New Rochelle, New York – so it was easy to imagine being *in* the book. And riding too fast in a car with my cousin, who wasn't really my cousin, because June wasn't really my aunt.

When was my mother born?

It was either 1930 or 1931; it depends on whether she was illegitimate or not.

2.
My father mentioned that your eyes lit up, honey.

He always says things like that.

It makes me think that he

a) recognizes that you have eyes.
b) notices that they light up.

You know, the fact that my father notices that that my boyfriend's eyes light up (like something in a movie) makes me want to forgive him for being, well, my father.

3.
My father told a great story or two about my grandfather. He thinks they're just good stories, but as far as I'm concerned a lot of the

problems with my family originate with my grandfather. My father crashed the car and it wasn't his fault and my grandfather said, "Son, here's $20. Take the money to the police station. I hope that's enough to pay the fine. If it's not, then you'll have to go to go jail." My father didn't have money of his own and he believed my grandfather and he was very scared. Apparently, my grandfather and the judge had made a deal, so the twenty was enough. To me, this is the most despicable of all behaviours. There's Abu Ghraib prison and there's Hitler and then there's my grandfather – who might as well have been pulling the wings off flies when he tortured my father.

4.
Ever since Eloise threw up her taco at Chili's I haven't been able to look at her the same way.

5.
It strikes terror in my heart when my uncle says, "I don't mind that you're addicted to cheese crackers, I mean you could be addicted to so many other things."

6.
They mentioned the word "penis" at least four times when I was watching TV with my aunt and uncle. My aunt said, "We didn't need to hear that."

7.
My Dad asked how I met you. It was the sweetest thing – next to seeing the light in your eyes.

8.
I didn't bring back any cheese crackers for my sister. I'm mad at her because she ate all my cheese crackers last time.

9.

Lois and Fran gave me a frying pan.

10.

Dinah has two kids and so does Stephanie. Jane has three kids. Meg has two (but one is adopted). Gwen also has two kids. So does Cliff, and Chris has three. I don't have any kids.

11.

My father used the phrase "imaginary aunt" to describe my grandfather's sister. "Does that mean he made her up?" I asked. "No, it just means that she was his friend, not his actual sister," he said. This made me think about words and how much more interesting they are than reality. Like Sebastian Melmoth, or iteration, or aporia, or willing dusk, or *the enmity between them froze in a kind of silent stasis that paralyzed every particle of affection* (if affection were a particle). Or, not having you here and talking with you on the phone when your boss is waiting on your end and my parents are waiting on mine isn't like talking at all, more like yelling down a vast white tunnel – you have to yell carefully so you don't get spittle on the walls.

12.

I'm awfully glad you found a boyfriend for our cat.
But remember . . .

a) She's fixed and can't have his babies.
b) Even though he's prettier than her we can't kill her, we just can't. I don't have time to explain it now, but we can't.

13.

This is the final thing I remember about the trip to my dad's. We got into a conversation about piercings, and everybody agreed that they couldn't understand why, I mean why, people would *do* that. And the tongue piercings! And then Alyson Carthosy said, "What about the navel piercings?" And then they went on about that . . . But since I do have a navel piercing I tried not to go on about how awful they were, although I did mention that they do tend to get infected.

I just wanted to feel like I was a part of everything.

IT'S SOMETHING I LEARNED A LONG TIME AGO PLAYING CHESS WITH DOMINIC

Just because he experienced it with me, doesn't necessarily make it his. Driving up Highway Six and seeing the Texas Grill, remembering Ian remarked on it. Not a remark, really, just a mumble. And now we're entering Freelton, where he remarked on the general store, and boy but I'm glad that his tests came back negative. But back to Dominic – after I played chess with him and we listened to Debussy's *La Mer* he asked, "Can you hear that trumpet?" And I did, I did, boy did I hear that trumpet. Then I went home and listened to *La Mer* over and over and all I could do was think of Dominic and cry. He had it, he had my personality; it was still hovering there, somewhere, above his chessboard. Then years of therapy (I'm not a homosexual – but I am, really) just to find out that Dominic doesn't own my personality – I do. And then I'm sitting watching the students acting in my play, and then they are crying, after it's all over, so much like Dominic and me. But for me it's not over because I carry me, inside . . . until I breathe my last. And there's some movie that says your soul weighs six pounds and it floats away when you die, making you markedly lighter. A new kind of diet. So, I'm reminding myself that Ian doesn't own the bus ride to Guelph just because we experienced it together. Even though now, when I ride alone and see the Texas Grill, I think of him.

PARKER POSEY

Parker Posey is highly underrated
my boyfriend looks just like her in drag
but that's not why I'm saying this

How do I love thee Parker Posey
the way you throw your body around
the way I can see every thought that goes through your head
most of all your anger
your seething, uncontrollable, non-feminine anger
that lets itself loose in such alarming ways

I love that your voice is too hard and flat for your pretty smile
which is just a bit too big for your mouth
– everything about you is too big, except your body
like Mary Tyler Moore on drugs

I love it when you steal the boss's pens in *Clockwatchers*
I love it when you dance stoned in *Party Girl*
I love it when you give it to Tori Spelling in *The House of Yes*
I love you Parker Posey, because I am you

We are superior, awkward, lonely in a crowded room
always on the lookout for a drug that will kill our next child
    in vitro
always hungrily kissing because we seriously lack self-esteem
and highly, highly underrated

IAN'S GETTING DRUNK

Ian's getting drunk
It's time to hide Maggie and your feelings
Quick, get a pot so he can throw up
Quick, warn the neighbours because he's gonna start groaning
Ian's getting drunk
Turn up the music to cover his screams
but don't try to touch him – he won't let you
"Stay away from me!" he'll say
"everything will be fine if you just don't touch me!"
Ian's getting drunk
and the Christmas decorations aren't up yet
so I might as well put them up now
Look, he's telling me how much he loves me
Look, he's telling me how beautiful my penis is
(Even if it's not all that big)
Look, he's telling me he finds me attractive
he couldn't possibly go out with someone unattractive
– that would be beneath him
Look, he's hugging me
(Actually he's just falling)
Ian's getting drunk
At first it's just like Tom on Ecstasy
but then it gets a lot grimmer
Uh, oh – he feels so sick
Hide, behind the stairs
Or beneath them
Hide inside the stairs
Ian's getting drunk

ODE TO IAN

Ian, my every waking moment a crying shame
that you recommended that I stay at the Hotel American
    in Montreal
shows how cruel you are
true, when I met you I was blinded by the brightness in your eyes
I know now that behind them lurks a very angry boy
who would eat the flesh off a corpse
if it was easier and not quite so bad for his health
the amazing thing is that I love you, still
maybe because, walking down the street today, I said to Ed
"When you hang around straight people
it makes you stop complaining about gay people doesn't it?
I mean gay people are horrible
but straight people are ten times as horrible"
and Ed said (I'm not kidding)
"Gee, what a tortured universe you live in"
Yes, I do, and you share it with me, Ian
I know you won't like me mentioning Shakespeare
but when they lock up Malvolio
he's alone, and crazy in the dark
I'm crazy in the dark
but I have you

TO THE BOY WHO SITS BY THE POOL

There is a wealth of hope in your arrogance
and in the tightness of your bathing suit

It was the summer when all the Montreal boys
wore underwear that said "Home of the Brave"
and Ed and I sat at the Adonis
remembering Peter Brawley

It was better when he was there
now, the strippers seem to be trying too hard
or not trying at all
which comes down to pretty much the same thing

Are you a stripper, boy by the pool?
I really love the fact that your every move says
"I would never ever fuck you, you ugly old toad!"

Because I don't expect you to fuck me
and in your certainty lies
all the tragic beauty of the world

OLD MAN

His face hasn't changed much
that is, he's still attractive
and he says the same about me

"You don't look that different," he says
– he means when we were lovers

He is so kind and I really do love him

I guess it's the father thing
that won't go away
meaning everything
he says makes me angry

"Do you drive?" he asks

"No, I never learned," I say
which is something odd about me
something people never understand
"but the commute is really nice –
I like taking the bus"

I'm practically begging for a firm
supportive response, but no

And since now we both have new lovers
he must talk about how perfect his relationship is
"I find that as I grow older
we become closer"

I forget for a moment how perfect he is
how imperfect I am
I will always be the honest son

because, okay, fuck it, age
hasn't brought me closer to my lover
only raised new problems

Old man, I'm not perfect like you
my boyfriend isn't either
and I don't deal with everything
with perfect equanimity
perhaps that's why I'm an writer and you're not
I'm fucking crazy and imperfect, okay?

But believe it or not I still love you
– it's a Dad thing

KEY WEST REGRET

I kissed you at the end of the southernmost pier in America
I swam naked in the hotel bar pool
I got all dressed up in drag
and had my ass slapped by a guy from Ohio
I bought poppers for the first time in a year
and then sucked off the oldest living ex-pro in Key West
(he was almost living)
I hung out in the dirty video room at Island House
for an entire rainy afternoon
but I wouldn't have sex with anybody there
because they were all so ugly and from Indiana
I realized how easy it was to have sex with thousands of others
(or not) and still love you best
I showed off my nipple ring and then jerked off with strangers
until my dick started to hurt and I went back to our hotel
to watch conservative television news (fair and impartial)
while waiting to kiss you goodnight
I had my cake and ate it too
I had everyone and I still have you

LAURA'S DREAM

One night she asks me how to get to Kennedy Station. I tell her. The next day she comes to rehearsal, crying.

"I had a really bad night," Laura says.

I ask Paul what the problem is. He's reticent.

It must be her first encounter with evil.

There's the usual academic explanation for Iago. No matter how much he prevaricates, explains, rationalizes, it's not his childhood. He's not in love with Desdemona, or Othello. His endless yammering is only "motive-hunting of motiveless malignity."

Just a few days later, Laura is bouncy. Her round face is troubled, but it's merely a fluffy bunny cloud today, not a thunderstorm. "I had the most awful dream last night," she chirps.

"What?" I ask.

"It's too complicated, but it was really, well, detailed."

"Did you eat cheese last night?"

"Yeah, I did. Nachos."

"Well that's why you had the dream."

"What do you mean?"

"That's what happens when you eat cheese late at night. I used to think it was a deep psychological thing, then I realized I get nightmares every time I eat cheese right before going to bed. It's because your stomach has a very hard time digesting it."

Laura looks at me skeptically. She thinks I'm kidding.

But it's her first, real, lesson.

WHY I WOULD RATHER CHAT WITH A HAMILTON CRACK WHORE THAN AN OLD RICH TORONTO LADY WITH A LAP DOG

1. Teeth: The Hamilton Ho doesn't have enough; the Toronto Lady has too many.

2. Voice: The Hamilton Ho has no voice because of the drugs; the Toronto Lady because of the cigarettes. Both sport a deep, scratchy rasp.

3. Overall appearance: The Hamilton Ho is a bit scary. There's something wrong with the way she walks; her drug problem has probably affected her legs. Her hair is scraggly. But other than that, she looks pretty much the same as the Toronto Lady – both, after all, favour the wild animal prints usually associated with women half their age, many years ago.

4. Ethics and Morality: The Toronto Lady of course has no problem buying foods grown by oppressed peoples, and is irritated when you point this out. She is also a racist, and if you point this out she gives you a tired "Oh please." She just doesn't have the time or energy any more to worry about such things and, after all, how does it really affect her? The Hamilton Ho, on the other hand, is sympathetic to pretty well everybody.

5. Crankiness: Here the ho has it all over the lady, mainly because she will simply tell you "I'm in a fucking lousy mood today because my feet hurt and they're trying to take my kid away from me again." After that, it's easy to have a relaxed chat. The Toronto Lady has a veneer of icy false-friendliness which masks a deep frustration with existence that is never, ever, mitigated by time.

6. Meeting Places: Ho prefers Tim Ho's or CD Martini's; lady the deli underneath the cinema at the Manulife Centre. I much prefer

Tim Ho's; CD Martini's is a bit dangerous, but the conversations you overhear make for twice the fun.

7. Homophobia: With the Hamilton Ho you can talk frankly about sex (last night's sex, in fact). I wouldn't try that with the Toronto Lady; she is liable to choke on her goat cheese salad.

8. Considerateness: The ho is considerate. Because someone whose arms look like uncooked ground chuck is acutely aware of how painful life can actually be.

9. Money: The Hamilton Ho never has any, and as soon as she does, it's gone. If she did have some, however, she'd spend it on you. The lady is loaded but will never give you a penny. "How do you think the rich got that way?" she says.

10. Dependability: The Hamiltonian is really there for you sometimes; and not at all, at other times. The Torontonian is too busy coveting other women's designer handbags to ever really sympathize – but she always turns up on time.

POEM FOR KEITH'S BIRTHDAY

1. Call him.
2. Date him.
3. Fuck him.
4. Tell yourself you'll forget him.
5. Have trouble forgetting him.
6. Cry a lot over him.
7. Masturbate to his picture.
8. Call him again, but tell him you're sorry for being
   such a pest.
9. Hang out outside his house.
10. Confront him on the street.
11. Get yelled at by him.
12. Collapse on the pavement, crying.
13. Call Laura Cowell and tell her all about what happened.
14. Go home and create a performance piece about him.
15. Pee on the stage. Pee for him!
16. Fuck lots and lots of others, thinking only of him.
17. Wake up in an alley with your jockstrap around your neck,
    thinking only of him.
18. Sneak into his house and steal his dirty underwear.
19. Go home and fall asleep, contented somehow,
    with the underwear in your mouth.
20. Start all over again, this time with someone else.

PHOTOS FOR MY FAMILY: THE CAPTIONS I NEVER SENT

1.

This is the upstairs den / movie room. Do you like the posters? Ian and I like to curl up and watch movies in here. I'm standing beside the big screen projector. The poster "This is the way trouble came to Johnny Trouble" features Carolyn Jones climbing through the window. There's a cute guy on the bed. The poster represents my life. I'm Carolyn Jones and all the men I've ever met are the guy lying above the bed. His armpits are showing. I love to lick armpits.

2.

This is the upstairs bathroom. The mirror is dirty. Sorry. There's a picture of a bulldog wearing a sailor cap because Ian is fond of men with bad teeth. Did you know I have a huge space between my front teeth?

3.

This is Ian telling you not to go into his room. He's making a funny face. You wouldn't want to go in there because he's very messy and everything in the room is sexual, that is, if it's not an Elephant or something to do with *Star Wars* or Wonder Woman. Ian is making a pornographic movie about *Star Wars* right now. It's something you should never, ever, under any circumstance, see.

4.

This is the top of the stairway looking down into the main floor. My room is to the left. Ian put a red star on my door because I am one.

5.

This is our front hall. That's the bench you gave us, under the coats. Ian gave me the toothless monkey for our anniversary. It's one of those presents you don't ask questions about. But I did. He told me he gave it to me because I was worried that he would leave me for a toothless Hamilton man. (Or, more specifically, a toothless Hamilton monkey.) He promised never to do that.

6.
This is looking the other way from the front door into the hallway. That's Maggie on the stairs. You have to look closely because she matches the stairs. Ian hates her and wants to kill her. Really. I know we joke about it but the truth is he wants to kill my cat. I love him anyway.

7.
This is one view of the library / den at the front of the house. We have lots of plants in here. The painting of the nude boy on the wall was done by the father of one of Ian's best friends who died of AIDS.

8.
This is another view of the library / den. It's the most normal room in the house, which is frightening.

9.
This is a picture of the next room, which is now the costume room / hairdressing salon. I managed not to get the giant dildo in the picture. I hope I didn't miss anything else incriminating.

10.
This is another view of the costume room / hairdressing room. Ian is about to cut his father's hair. That's a picture of Britney Spears on the back wall. Doesn't Ian look like her? He used to want to be her, but I think he's pretty much grown out of it.

11.

This is the Tintin mural Ian painted for the living room wall. It's from a French comic book. Tintin never really visited the land of the drag queens, but we like to pretend he did.

12.

This is the back of the living room and the kichen. It's the only picture I could give you because just to the right is a painting of a giant bunny masturbating his huge cock. We thought you'd prefer to look at the kitchen this way.

13.

Here's a view of the house from the kitchen looking up to the front hall. That's our magnificently stocked bar. Ian got very drunk last week for the first time, with me that is, and it was very traumatic. He screamed a lot and threw up and talked about all the bad experiences he's had and how much he loved me. I guess that's just all part of being in a relationship.

ROMANCE

Nothing is more romantic than promiscuous sex
a different man every night
the one with the beard and piercing eyes who called me baby
the one with the boy's face
most of them want me to submit
but sometimes I make them

It's like the view in San Francisco
when we climbed the hill
and suddenly: a whole new vista

I get it every day arriving in Hamilton
the train comes out from under the bridge
and there you are
and the bay sits silent and deep (I think)
and there are birds and you can't even see the factories

And then there's the smallest, thinnest point of land
where the water practically creates an island

It comes suddenly too
but every time it's like the first time

And it's like love, I think, being
where the water's all around you
and you might fall in

Or when my boyfriend's passionately irrational outbursts
suddenly shipwreck me
as if God spit me out
and the unshaven faces of men
discover me for the first time

THE PERFORMANCE

You tiny mitre saw
you little mortar board
you obsequious flea

You attacked my boyfriend
and said we don't have a real relationship
"What's the use of having a boyfriend
if you don't fuck him?" you said

Well, what's the use of being a homosexual
if you don't talk about it now and then?
meanwhile, you're sucking off boys at That Place
and waiting for Mr. Right
your hypocrisy is matched only by the guesthouse I'm staying in

I stupidly said you have a sexy ass
and that I was once attracted to you, years ago,
when you used to leave witty plays on my desk
and then act surprised I contacted you about them

You are a bad mini-modern sculpture in the neo-mannerist style
and an aging queer couple that owns a tasteless B & B
you are the theatre, which means you are certainly charming
but terribly, terribly small
and I can't believe I was ever attracted
to your furry little legs for even five minute minutes

There is a shruggingness about you

If only you weren't talented

For Christ's sake, could you just write
a fucking *gay* play
and then shut up already?

You are the white sheets laid out by a disapproving landlady
and I am the shit stains that convicted Wilde

I am certain of your duplicity as I am of Handel's homosexuality
and yet you were charming to spend a day with
rarely do I meet anyone who can skip
from one topic to another so effortlessly
or endure my mountains of conversation

You are gay; in every sense of the word, except the important one
but even your furious refusal to be pigeonholed
    may yet prove superficial

If we do not revel in superficiality we are lost
effete in exactly the wrong way
if we don't get ourselves very dirty and lick the grease
then we are nothing more than those dilettantes with bad hair
and breath who hang out at the end of openings
or the openings of ends
aching for release

I take it back
when I said I was attracted to you
I was merely acting

QUEER MANIFESTO (WITH APOLOGIES TO TRISTAN TZARA)

(The signatories practice
fellatio, cunnilingus, mutual masturbation, anal and vaginal intercourse with human beings of various sizes, shapes, colours, dis- and other abilities and ages, but the signatories refuse to be assigned by the medical and psychiatric powers that be who are working in their labs, testing our sperm and cunt juices, diligently, long into the night, trying to figure out who and what we are – we refuse to be assigned any specific sexuality by these white coated MADMEN!)

QUEER EXCITES EVERYTHING

QUEER knows everything. QUEER spits everything out.

But . . .

HAS QUEER EVER SPOKEN TO YOU?
1. about being nice
2. about obeying
3. about repressing your feelings
4. about repressing your thoughts
5. about repressing your lusts
6. about worrying about your sexual object choice
7. about the importance of wearing pants
8. about being good
9. about following orders
10. about how to make a million
11. about being a hypocrite
12. about lying
13. about the past
14. about the ultimate hypocrisy called marriage
15. about trying not to make any trouble for anyone

16. about trying to forget what's bugging you
17. about shutting up
18. about being just like everyone else
19. about sexual addiction
20. about having too much fun
21. about being an exemplary citizen
22. about all the boring SHIT that makes you want to slit your fucking wrists?

NEVER NEVER NEVER

QUEER doesn't speak. QUEER has no fixed idea.
QUEER doesn't catch flies.

THE GOVERNMENT IS OVERTURNED.
By what?

By QUEER

THE GAY LIBERATION MOVEMENT IS DEAD.
Of what?

Of QUEER

JOY is rampant.
Why?

Blame Queer.
Someone quits their job and dances naked in the streets. Why?
Queer.
A molester puts his dick in his pants cuz he can get
better sex with his fuckbuddy at home. Why?
Queer.
If you want to understand who you are

if you want to find in your sexuality again
if all of a sudden your head begins to crackle with laughter
and if you find all your ideas useless and ridiculous, know that

QUEER IS BEGINNING TO SPEAK TO YOU

advertising wants you to buy more iPods iMacs and iMachines
i i i i i i i i i i i i i i i i i i i i i i i i i i i i i i i i i i i i i i i i i i i i i i i

WHAT DOES QUEER DO?
religion wants you sit your itchy ass down in a pew
for hours upon boring hours until you want to scream
WHAT DOES QUEER DO?
fashion wants you to buy more ridiculous expensive clothes
WHAT DOES QUEER DO?
political correctness wants you to worry about saying the wrong
    thing
WHAT DOES QUEER DO?
old fashioned feminism wants you to make sure
    you're not penetrated
WHAT DOES QUEER DO?
gay liberation separates the men from the women
WHAT DOES QUEER DO?
body fascism wants you to starve yourself
WHAT DOES QUEER DO?
the United States of America wants you to hate the world
WHAT DOES QUEER DO?
fundamentalism asks you to hate your body
and cut off your clit and foreskin and save them in a bottle
WHAT DOES QUEER DO?
WHAT DOES QUEER DO?

50 CANADIAN LOONIES

THAT WOULD BE WORTH A LOT MORE IF OUR ECONOMY WAS NOT SO
SYMBIOTICALLY ATTACHED TO THE MAD OPPRESSIVE FASCISTIC
AMERICAN ONE DOWN UNDER

A 50 DOLLAR CANADIAN REWARD
to the person who finds the best
way to explain QUEER to us

QUEER passes everything through a new net.
QUEER is the bitterness which opens its laugh on all that which has
been made verboten, unmentionable, shocking, unimportant,
repressible in a culture which would leave you dickless,
cuntless, and loveless.
It says: There is Sex and Multiple Nameless Sexualities
who cares what they are called
and yes contrary to popular opinion
YOU DO HAVE A BODY AND THE TWO SPIRITED GOD WHO RUNS THIS
DAMN UNIVERSE MADE IT FOR YOUR PLEASURE BECAUSE SHE'S
SOMETHING OF A WHORE HERSELF!

QUEER has always existed
The Holy Virgin was already a QUEER

REMEMBER
QUEER IS NEVER RIGHT
OR WRONG
when it comes to sexuality there is no objective morality
there is only CONSENT CONSENT
say it with me
CONSENT!

Citizens, comrades, ladies, gentlemen, drag queens, kings, whores, perverts, fuckbuddies, online chat room porn addicts, those who like to do it doggy style or on a mattress on sale at Zellers during slow hours, because at Zellers you can always get the over 55 discount

Beware of forgeries!

Imitators of QUEER
want to present QUEER
as something radical and dangerous
that will threaten your very way of life

DON'T WORRY: THAT'S WHAT IT IS!

SERIOUSLY FOLKS

You are presented today, in a distinctly boring and careful and unimaginative form, a so-called new neo-conservative, more acceptable and palatable and politically correct gay and lesbian sexuality that features sexlessness and hypocrisy and church-going and baby-making and coupledom and buying couches in the suburbs so that ultimately gay and lesbian have become the same as straight, except for being more hypocritical and even more prone to wearing leisure suits

THIS IS DOGMATISM AND PRETENTIOUS IMBECILITY

SAY IT WITH ME
QUEER IS GOOD
SAY IT WITH ME
QUEER IS GREAT
SAY IT WITH ME
SAY IT LOUDER
FUCK!
SAY IT PROUDLY
WE'RE ALL FUCKIN' QUEER!

ACKNOWLEDGEMENTS

I would like to thank Michael Holmes for his endless support and editorial wisdom over the (many) years.